SNAPSEED

PHOTO EDITING APPLICATION

HARVEY SPECTER

Snapseed is an iOS and Android photo-editing tool that allows users to enhance photographs and apply digital filters. Nik Software created it, and it is now owned by Google.

Contents

Foreword

Snapseed is without a doubt one of the best photo editing application available. If you're not convinced by the features offered in simple editing software and don't want to wade through the complexities of a more professional photo editing tool, this is the option for you. Then the Snapseed app is just what you need.

Preface

To put it another way, the Snapseed gives you access to all of the capabilities and high-quality editing that you'd find in professional photo editing software. However, you won't find the extra complications that you might find in professional programs. As a result, it's the ideal simple photo editing program for producing professional shots and images.

Snapseed is an iOS and Android photo-editing tool that allows users to enhance photographs and apply digital filters. Nik Software created it, and it is now owned by Google.

Snapseed was first released on the iPad in June 2011, and it was selected Apple's iPad App of the Year 2011. Nik announced Snapseed for the iPhone in August 2011, following the success of the iPad version. Snapseed for Microsoft Windows was later revealed on February 27, 2012.

Snapseed was released on Android in December 2012, following Google's acquisition, and the PC version of Snapseed was discontinued.

Nik released Snapseed 2.0 for iOS and Android on April 9, 2015, with additional tools, capabilities, and a redesigned user interface.

Reasons to use Snapseed.

- Free!
- Professional-grade presets and tools are included.
- Amateur and professional photographers alike use it.
- User-friendly
- RAW files can be edited
- To edit images, simply swipe your finger across the sliders.
- There are no advertisements.

Common feature

- Edit photos with swiping gestures
- Variety of effects
- Color and contrast adjustments done automatically
- Save user's editing history
- Use combination of filters as well as default filters
- A variety of filters Eg: Drama, Grunge, Vintage, Center-focus, Frames and Tilt-ashift

- Import RAW images
- New filters such as, lens blur, glamor glow, HDR scape and noir
- Directly share images on social media

Acknowledgements

We are a devoted and passionate team that is more concerned with bringing your attention to the Snapseed App-related problems in order to broaden your basic comprehension of your App-related inquiries while also providing you with the fundamental instructions for App installation.

CHAPTER ONE

SNAPSEED FOR PC

Whether it's selfies, candid's, or landscapes, photography is one of the most popular hobbies today. Obtaining high-quality images for a variety of media is a top priority for a big number of people. While shooting the perfect shot is key, altering the photo before sharing it on other networks is also necessary. With their vast number of beauty tools and filters, there are a plethora of photo-editing programs and software to meet this requirement. Snapseed is one of the most popular and powerful apps in its category.

Enter Caption

Snapseed is a powerful photo-editing program that is both easy to use and install. It is a component of Google's picture technology. This application was acquired by Google from Nik Software, the creators of

Snapseed, and is equipped with a wide range of editing tools, plug-ins, and photo filters. Even after the acquisition, Google has continued to add a huge variety of tools including high dynamic range (HDR) filters to expand the application's photo-editing flexibility. It's a popular Instagram alternative that's also highly recommended for professional photographers.

Snapseed Apk includes everything from beginner tools to sophisticated features for professional photographers and photo editors. The controls are also easily positioned, and the UI is slick and easy to use for everyone. Overall, it's a photographer's dream come true when it comes to photo editing and retouching.

CHAPTER TWO

SNAPSEED FOR PC (continued...)

Reasons to use Snapseed on PC

- The installation process is quick, and the configuration is simple.
- Easy to use.
- There will be no more battery constraints.
- There will be no more annoying phone calls or text messages.
- There are no limitations on mobile data usage.
- Possibility of obtaining a full-screen and wide-screen experience.
- User-friendliness

CHAPTER THREE

HOW TO INSTALL SNAPSEED TO PC

How to install Snapseed on PC

Snapseed is a free app available for Android and iOS. The procedure for PC is also straightforward and is described in detail below:

- Click here to get Bluestacks or another high-quality emulator for your PC. After it has finished downloading, you should install the application on your computer. Also, provide an emulator the permissions it needs to function properly.
- Open the emulator from its desktop or search icon once it has been installed and permissions have been granted.
- After the emulator has loaded, go to the Google Play Store or a web browser and search for 'Snapseed.'
- Simply choose one of the two sources to get the Snapseed app. Then, directly inside the emulator, install the application.
- After the application has been installed, go to the main menu and click on the Snapseed icon to start using it on your computer.
- To get started with Snapseed, the program will ask for some basic information and your Google account credentials.
- Once you've completed the basic setup, you can start working on your photos and recreating them in whatever way you choose.

CHAPTER FOUR

SNAPSEED FOR IOS

Snapseed is a powerful photo-editing app for iOS that you can use anywhere. Simply take a picture using your iPhone's camera, or select one from your camera roll, and use the numerous editing and effects options to turn it into a high-quality print.

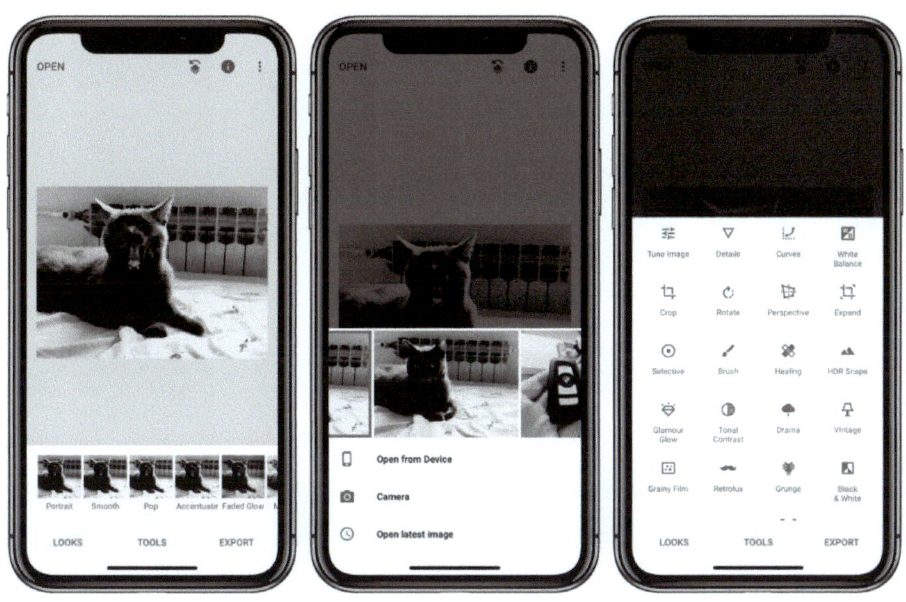

Enter Caption

Snapseed is simple to use: simply hit the Camera icon to shoot a new picture, select one from your photo library, or paste a previously copied image. Automatic and Selective Adjust, Tune Image, Straighten, Crop, Details, Black & White, and Frames are just a few of the image altering features available in the program. Each tool comes with its own set of instructions, which mainly consist of swiping your fingertips left or right, up, and down, and so on. Some of it takes a little skill, but we were editing our photo and changing color contrasts and brightness in no time. You can easily share your edited image on numerous social media platforms, including Google+, Twitter, and, of course, Facebook.

Snapseed is the app for you if you want to elevate your iPhone photos to the next level. We recommend this capable photo-editing tool to all users.

CHAPTER FIVE

HOW TO INSTALL SNAPSEED TO IPHONE

How to Install

Snapseed is now available for free download for your iOS device. Follow the instructions below. First download the Snapseed APK file, after which the rest of the process is simple.

Step 01: To begin, you must first download the Snapseed APK file, as previously stated. You can do so by using the reputable download link given. It is important to download it directly from the internet.

Step 02: Open your device's settings folder. Then you must enable the option for unknown sources. Follow the instructions below to enable the unknown source option.

Settings > Security settings > Enable unknown sources.

Step 03: Then you must close all of the open windows. After that, go to the download folder on your device.

Step 04: Now you must launch the Snapseed APK file that you have downloaded. Start the installation by tapping on it. Accept the terms and conditions of your application to continue the procedure.

Step 05: Finally, the procedure has been completed. Start using Snapseed and Enjoy!

CHAPTER SIX

WHAT'S NEW ON SNAPSEED IOS

Snapseed is a capable iPhone and iPad photo editing software. While the Photos apps on iOS include basic picture editing software, Snapseed does everything better and offers more functionality.

Snapseed is a good combination of amateur and professional photo editing. There are standard level adjustments for exposure, contrast, and highlights, as well as a slew of filters for easy tweaking.

You don't have to worry about losing the original photo because all modifications are non-destructive. You may reverse your alterations or return to the original photo if you don't like how they ended out. A spot removal brush is available for advanced users to assist them eliminate small defects from their images. It's a useful function that might assist you in fine-tuning your shot before posting it on social media.

So, what's new in Snapseed,

- Healing, Brush, Structure, HDR, and Perspective are among the 29 tools and filters available.
- JPG and RAW files are supported.
- You may save your own looks and use them in fresh images later.
- Brush with a selective filter
- All styles can be fine-tuned with pinpoint accuracy.

CHAPTER SEVEN

SNAPSEED FOR ANDROID

There are a lot of photo editing applications on the Play Store, but only a few of them provide you the tools you need to edit photos like an expert on your smartphone. Snapseed, a Google-developed photo-editing tool, contains all of the features you're looking for in a photo-editing program. You can edit your photos and make them great for posting on social networking sites with just a few touches and a little understanding. The user interface is straightforward and intuitive.

Enter Caption

Snapseed has up to 29 tools and filters, including a healing tool to cover blemishes, a brush tool, and hdr, among others. It can open both JPEG and RAW files. This lens blur tool is ideal for portrait photography. Face pose feature, which fixes the pose of portraits based on 3d models, is also available.

CHAPTER EIGHT

HOW TO INSTALL SNAPSEED TO ANDROID

How to Install

Snapseed is now available for Android users to download for free. Follow the steps outlined below. After downloading the Snapseed APK file, the remainder of the procedure is straightforward.

Step 1: As previously said, you must first download the Snapseed APK file. You can do so by following the provided download link above.

Step 2: Go to the settings folder on your smartphone. The option for unknown sources must then be enabled. To enable the unknown source option, follow the steps below.

Settings > Security settings > Enable unknown sources.

Step 3: Finally, all of the open windows must be closed. After that, browse to your device's download folder.

Step 04: Now it's time to run the Snapseed APK file you just downloaded. By clicking on it, you can begin the installation process. To proceed with the procedure, accept the terms and conditions of your application.

Step 05: Start editing your photos and have fun!

CHAPTER NINE

WHAT'S NEW ON SNAPSEED FOR ANDROID

What's New

Users of Snapseed may edit photos with swiping gestures to choose from a variety of effects and enhancements. Users can also choose to have color and contrast adjusted "automatically." Snapseed can save a user's editing history and return them to any previous activity. Using the basic filters and editing features, it can also create and save filter combinations. Drama, Grunge, Vintage, Center-focus, Frames, and a Tilt-shift are among the special effects and filters available (which resizes photos). Users can also import RAW pictures for higher-quality editing. Snapseed 2.0 added new filters such lens blur, glamour glow, HDR scape, and noir, as well as a redesigned tools section with a more user-friendly layout. Users can share the photographs immediately on social media sites such as Facebook and Instagram.

So, what's new in Snapseed,

- Healing, Brush, Structure, HDR, and Perspective are among the 29 tools and filters available.
- Both JPG and RAW files are supported.
- Save your personal looks and use them in future images.
- Brush with a selective filter
- All styles can be fine-tuned with pinpoint accuracy.

9 798886 841374

Printed by Libri Plureos GmbH in Hamburg,
Germany